CLASSICAL SOLOS FOR TRUMPET

ONLINE MEDIA INCLUDED
Audio Recordings
Printable Piano Accompaniments

PLAYBACK+
Speed • Pitch • Balance • Loop

15 Easy Solos for Contest and Performance
Arranged by Philip Sparke

T0083361

TITLE	PAGE
Waltz	2
Chorale (Now praise, my soul, the Lord)	3
Humming Song (from *Album for the Young*)	4
Gymnopédie No. 1	5
I'm Called Little Buttercup (from *HMS Pinafore*)	6
Study (Op. 37, No. 3)	7
Minuet (Z. 649)	8
Theme and Variation (from *Sonatina No. 3*)	9
Northern Song (from *Album for the Young*)	10
Two German Dances (from *12 German Dances, D. 420*)	11
Watchman's Song (from *Lyric Pieces, Op. 12*)	12
Gavotte	13
Vien quà, Dorina bella	14
Minuet (from *Notebook for Anna Magdalena Bach*)	15
The Prince of Denmark's March	16
B♭ Tuning Notes	

To access recordings and PDF accompaniments visit:
www.halleonard.com/mylibrary

Enter Code
7860-3776-0409-3036

ISBN 978-170516-742-7

HAL•LEONARD®

World headquarters, contact:
Hal Leonard
7777 West Bluemound Road
Milwaukee, WI 53213
Email: info@halleonard.com

In Europe, contact:
Hal Leonard Europe Limited
1 Red Place
London, W1K 6PL
Email: info@halleonardeurope.com

In Australia, contact:
Hal Leonard Australia Pty. Ltd.
4 Lentara Court
Cheltenham, Victoria, 3192 Australia
Email: info@halleonard.com.au

WALTZ

B♭ TRUMPET

MORITZ VOGEL
Arranged by PHILIP SPARKE

00870095

CHORALE

Now praise, my soul, the Lord

B♭ TRUMPET

JOHANN SEBASTIAN BACH
Arranged by PHILIP SPARKE

HUMMING SONG

from *Album for the Young*

B♭ TRUMPET

ROBERT SCHUMANN
Arranged by PHILIP SPARKE

GYMNOPÉDIE NO. 1

B♭ TRUMPET

ERIK SATIE
Arranged by PHILIP SPARKE

I'M CALLED LITTLE BUTTERCUP

from *HMS Pinafore*

B♭ TRUMPET

SIR ARTHUR SULLIVAN
Arranged by PHILIP SPARKE

00870095

STUDY

Op. 37, No. 3

B♭ TRUMPET

HENRY LEMOINE
Arranged by PHILIP SPARKE

MINUET

(Z. 649)

B♭ TRUMPET

HENRY PURCELL
Arranged by PHILIP SPARKE

THEME AND VARIATION

from *Sonatina No. 3*

B♭ TRUMPET

THOMAS ATTWOOD
Arranged by PHILIP SPARKE

NORTHERN SONG

from *Album for the Young*

B♭ TRUMPET

ROBERT SCHUMANN
Arranged by PHILIP SPARKE

TWO GERMAN DANCES

from *Twelve German Dances, D. 420*

B♭ TRUMPET

FRANZ SCHUBERT
Arranged by PHILIP SPARKE

00870095

WATCHMAN'S SONG

from *Lyric Pieces, Op. 12*

B♭ TRUMPET

EDVARD GRIEG
Arranged by PHILIP SPARKE

GAVOTTE

B♭ TRUMPET

JAN LADISLAV DUSSEK
Arranged by PHILIP SPARKE

VIEN QUÀ, DORINA BELLA

B♭ TRUMPET

ANTONIO BIANCHI
Transcribed by C. M. von WEBER
Arranged by PHILIP SPARKE

00870095

MINUET

from *Notebook for Anna Magdalena Bach*

B♭ TRUMPET

Attributed to **CHRISTIAN PETZOLD**
Arranged by PHILIP SPARKE

THE PRINCE OF DENMARK'S MARCH

from *Choice Lessons for the Harpsichord or Spinet*

B♭ TRUMPET

JEREMIAH CLARKE
Arranged by PHILIP SPARKE